MW01064400

Journal
A Guide to Self-Discovery and Growth

Susan E. Carrell, RN, LPC

Carrell Counseling Services
Allenspark, Colorado

Los Angeles | London | New Delhi
Singapore | Washington DC

Copyright © 2010 by SAGE Publications, Inc.

All rights reserved. No part of this book may be reproduced or utilized in any form or by any means, electronic or mechanical, including photocopying, recording, or by any information storage and retrieval system, without permission in writing from the publisher.

For information:

SAGE Publications, Inc.
2455 Teller Road
Thousand Oaks,
 California 91320
E-mail: order@sagepub.com

SAGE Publications India Pvt. Ltd.
B 1/I 1 Mohan Cooperative
 Industrial Area
Mathura Road, New Delhi 110 044
India

SAGE Publications Ltd.
1 Oliver's Yard
55 City Road
London EC1Y 1SP
United Kingdom

SAGE Publications Asia-Pacific Pte. Ltd.
33 Pekin Street #02-01
Far East Square
Singapore 048763

Printed in the United States of America.

This book is printed on acid-free paper.

10   11   12   13   14   10   9   8   7   6   5   4   3   2   1

Acquisitions Editor: Kassie Graves
Editorial Assistant: Veronica Novak
Production Editor: Karen Wiley
Copy Editor: Melinda Masson
Typesetter: C&M Digitals (P) Ltd.
Proofreader: Kristen Bergstad
Cover Designer: Candice Harman
Marketing Manager: Stephanie Adams

Contents

·····················
Journal Exercises
·····················

Introduction

This journal is for you alone. It is your private place to express your feelings, identify your hopes, and outline your dreams. You can practice being an artist, play around with being a poet, and try your skills as a writer.

This journal is not a diary! Diaries can be stressful because you are supposed to write in them every day. Write in your journal only when you want to. Journals are for self-expression, so use yours when you are glad, mad, sad, scared, lonely, guilty, or just plain bored.

A journal is your best friend in self-discovery. Go back to reread what you have written often. You may surprise yourself!

Most of all, don't judge yourself when you write or draw in your journal. Turn off that little voice in your head that criticizes your handwriting, how you say something, your sketches, and everything else. Let go and let it flow! Seriously, have fun.

1 Gratitude List

It's easy to forget the good stuff in life when things are hard. Keeping a gratitude list for several days or even a few weeks will help you remember how much you have to be grateful for. It can be a real attitude changer!

I am grateful for. . .

_____

_____

_____

_____

_____

_____

_____

_____

_____

_____

_____

_____

_____

_____

_____

_____

_____

_____

My thoughts...

2 My Poem

Whether you write poetry a lot or have never written a poem, there is a poet in you. See what happens when you put your feelings into a poem . . . or two, or three . . .

Title: _____

_____

_____

_____

_____

_____

_____

_____

_____

_____

_____

_____

_____

_____

_____

_____

_____

_____

_____

_____

_____

3 My Favorite Childhood Memory

Write about a favorite childhood memory. It might be a holiday or special trip with your family. It may be just an ordinary day that you remember with happy feelings. Your memory is a jewel in your personal treasure chest.

_____

_____

_____

_____

_____

_____

_____

_____

_____

_____

_____

_____

_____

_____

_____

_____

_____

_____

_____

_____

My Ideal
BOYFRIEND/
GIRLFRIEND

4 My "Ideal" Boyfriend or Girlfriend

What are the qualities you want in your ideal boyfriend or girlfriend? List all the characteristics that are important to you. Wonder if the person you are attracted to is really right for you? Just check your list!

1. _____

_____

_____

_____

2. _____

_____

_____

_____

3. _____

_____

_____

_____

4. _____

_____

_____

_____

5. _____

_____

_____

_____

6. _____

_____

_____

_____

7. _____

_____

_____

_____

8. _____

_____

_____

_____

9. _____

_____

_____

_____

10. _____

_____

_____

_____

Additional characteristics: _____

_____

_____

_____

_____

5 My Balance Sheet

Everyone has both good and bad character traits. You can celebrate your first-rate attributes and choose to work on the ones that are less positive. List your good and not-so-good character traits. Write about how you plan to work on improving your negative traits.

Good Traits	Not-So-Good Traits

Good Traits	Not-So-Good Traits
_____	_____
_____	_____
_____	_____
_____	_____
_____	_____
_____	_____
_____	_____
_____	_____
_____	_____
_____	_____
_____	_____
_____	_____
_____	_____
_____	_____

How I plan to work on my negative traits:

_____

_____

_____

_____

_____

_____

_____

_____

_____

_____

_____
_____
_____
_____
_____
_____
_____
_____
_____
_____
_____
_____
_____
_____
_____
_____
_____
_____
_____
_____
_____
_____
_____
_____

• •

6 My Friends

• •

Relationships with friends are superimportant, especially for teens. Friendship is give-and-take. Sometimes, people expect more from a friend than he or she is willing to give. Write about the qualities of a good friend (you can list the qualities if you want). Finally, answer this question: *Do I have these qualities?*

1. _____

_____

_____

_____

2. _____

_____

_____

_____

3 _____.

_____

_____

_____

4. _____

_____

_____

_____

5. _____

_____

_____

_____

6. _____

_____

_____

_____

7. _____

_____

_____

_____

8. _____

_____

_____

_____

9. _____

_____

_____

_____

10. _____

_____

_____

_____

Do I have these qualities? _____

_____

_____

_____

Much more may be happening in your life than you think. Record the events of your day in the time slots provided. You may want to do this for several days and then look back over your entries. Note: You have control over how you use your time. Are you happy with your choices? Write about your use of time and about changes you might want to make (if any).

7 a.m.–10 a.m.:

_____

_____

_____

_____

_____

_____

_____

_____

_____

_____

_____

_____

_____

_____

_____

10 a.m.–1 p.m.:

1 p.m.–4 p.m.:

4 p.m.–7 p.m.:

7 p.m.–10 p.m.

8 My Dream Job

It's not too early to start thinking about your career. Write about your dream job. What is it? Why are you drawn to it? Discuss your income. What will you need to do to prepare for your dream job? Be realistic; this could be the beginning of your career!

_____

_____

_____

_____

_____

_____

_____

_____

_____

_____

_____

_____

_____

_____

_____

_____

_____

_____

_____

_____

9 My Special Day

If you could design a perfect day, what would it look like? What would you do? Who would be with you? What would happen?

_____

_____

_____

_____

_____

_____

_____

_____

_____

_____

_____

_____

_____

_____

_____

_____

_____

_____

_____

_____

_____

10 My Favorite Teacher

Who is your favorite teacher ever? Why?

_____

_____

_____

_____

_____

_____

_____

_____

_____

_____

_____

_____

_____

_____

_____

_____

_____

_____

_____

_____

_____

My thoughts...

_____
_____
_____
_____
_____
_____
_____
_____
_____
_____
_____
_____
_____
_____
_____
_____
_____
_____
_____
_____
_____
_____
_____
_____
_____
_____
_____
_____
_____

11 My Family Portrait

We get many of our physical traits from our biological parents. We also get some of our personality traits from the family we grow up in. Some of these personality traits are positive; some are negative. If you recognize various personality traits in yourself and figure out where they came from, it will help you claim the positive ones and work on changing the negative ones. Consider the categories below and write your responses.

From my mom I get . . .

_____

_____

_____

_____

_____

_____

_____

_____

_____

_____

_____

_____

_____

_____

_____

From my dad I get . . .

From my siblings I get . . .

From my maternal grandparents I get . . .

_____

_____

_____

_____

_____

_____

_____

_____

_____

_____

_____

From my paternal grandparents I get . . .

_____

_____

_____

_____

_____

_____

_____

_____

_____

_____

_____

_____

From my aunt/uncle/cousin (any relative you would like to consider)
I get . . .

_____

_____

_____

_____

_____

_____

_____

_____

_____

_____

_____

_____

_____

_____

_____

_____

_____

_____

_____

_____

_____

_____

_____

_____

_____
_____
_____
_____
_____
_____
_____
_____
_____
_____
_____
_____
_____
_____
_____
_____
_____
_____
_____
_____
_____
_____
_____
_____
_____
_____

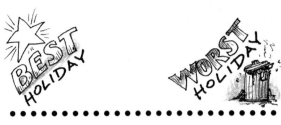

12 My Holidays

Holidays are important times. Write about your best and worst holiday ever.

_____ was my best holiday ever because . . .

_____

_____

_____

_____

_____

_____

_____

_____

_____

_____

_____

_____

_____

_____

_____

_____

_____

_____

_____ was my worst holiday ever because . . .

_____

_____

_____

_____

_____

_____

_____

_____

_____

_____

_____

_____

_____

_____

_____

_____

_____

_____

_____

_____

_____

_____

_____

_____

_____

_____

_____

_____

My thoughts...

13 Unfinished Sentences

Complete the following sentences and learn something about yourself!

My favorite food is . . .

_____

_____

_____

_____

_____

I have a crush on . . .

_____

_____

_____

_____

_____

I get embarrassed when . . .

_____

_____

_____

_____

_____

My favorite music group is . . .

_____

_____

_____

_____

_____

When I see someone mistreating someone else I . . .

_____

_____

_____

_____

_____

I get jealous when . . .

_____

_____

_____

_____

_____

I get really bored when . . .

_____

_____

_____

_____

_____

I love to . . .

_____

_____

_____

_____

_____

When someone snubs me I . . .

_____

_____

_____

_____

If I get mad enough, sometimes I . . .

_____

_____

_____

_____

I daydream about . . .

_____

_____

_____

_____

I'm happiest when . . .

_____

_____

_____

_____

14 My Biggest Worry

W rite about your biggest worry.

_____

_____

_____

_____

_____

_____

_____

_____

_____

_____

_____

_____

_____

_____

_____

_____

_____

_____

_____

_____

PRIORITIES

• •

15 My Priorities

• •

Many people don't know what is really important to them; you may not either. This exercise will help you discover your priorities. Just answer the questions below, and they will become clear.

What would you want to accomplish if you had 10 years to live?

_____

_____

_____

_____

_____

_____

_____

_____

_____

_____

_____

_____

_____

_____

_____

_____

_____

_____

What would you want to accomplish if you had 4 years to live?

_____
_____
_____
_____
_____
_____
_____
_____
_____
_____
_____
_____
_____
_____
_____
_____
_____
_____
_____
_____
_____
_____
_____
_____
_____
_____
_____

What would you want to accomplish if you had 1 year to live?

_____

_____

_____

_____

_____

_____

_____

_____

_____

_____

_____

_____

_____

_____

_____

_____

_____

_____

_____

_____

_____

_____

_____

_____

_____

_____

What would you want to accomplish if you had 6 months to live?

_____

_____

_____

_____

_____

_____

_____

_____

_____

_____

_____

_____

_____

_____

_____

_____

_____

_____

_____

_____

_____

_____

_____

_____

_____

_____

16 $$$$ Me and Money $$$$

You are in the process of developing a relationship with money. Write about how you manage your money in the categories that follow.

How I earn money:

_____

_____

_____

_____

_____

_____

How I spend money:

_____

_____

_____

_____

_____

_____

How I save money:

_____

_____

_____

_____

_____

_____

_____

_____

_____

_____

How I give money:

_____

_____

_____

_____

_____

_____

_____

_____

_____

_____

_____

My thoughts...

17 My Clothes

The clothes you wear and the way you dress are one way you express who you are. Complete the following statements to explore your relationship with fashion.

When I wear _____, I want people to think

_____

_____

_____

_____

_____

_____

_____.

When I wear _____, I want to think of myself as

_____

_____

_____

_____

_____

_____

_____

_____.

I wear _____

_____

_____

_____

_____

_____

_____ when I feel blah.

I wear _____

_____

_____

_____

_____

_____ when I feel outgoing.

I wear _____

_____

_____

_____

_____

_____ when I feel excited.

I wish I had the confidence to wear _____

_____

_____

_____

_____

_____ .

My favorite thing to wear is _____

because _____

_____

_____

_____

_____ .

• •

18 Exercise and Physical Fitness

• •

Exercise is essential to a healthy lifestyle. Think about your fitness level and complete the following statement. Follow up by writing about your satisfaction with your physical fitness. If you are not satisfied, what do you plan to do about it?

The place that exercise and physical fitness hold in my life is . . .

_____

_____

_____

_____

_____

_____

_____

_____

_____

_____

_____

_____

_____

_____

_____

_____

19 Storytelling and Creative Writing

Write a story and see where it goes.

Once upon a time, there was a boy/girl (it's probably more fun to choose your gender) who . . .

_____

_____

_____

_____

_____

_____

_____

_____

_____

_____

_____

_____

_____

_____

_____

_____

_____

My thoughts...

My FAVORITE Subject

20 Favorite Subject

W hat is your favorite subject in school? Why?

_____

_____

_____

_____

_____

_____

_____

_____

_____

_____

_____

_____

_____

_____

_____

_____

_____

_____

_____

_____

_____
_____
_____
_____
_____
_____
_____
_____
_____
_____
_____
_____
_____
_____
_____
_____
_____
_____
_____
_____
_____
_____
_____
_____
_____
_____
_____

21 You and God

What do you do that makes you feel closer to God?

_____

_____

_____

_____

_____

_____

_____

_____

_____

_____

_____

_____

_____

_____

_____

_____

_____

_____

_____

_____

My thoughts...

• •

22 My Peace and Comfort

• •

We all have the ability to soothe ourselves and make ourselves feel better, but we may not pay attention to all the things that bring us peace and comfort. Think about what helps you feel better when you are down or upset and list these items in the categories below.

Objects (like your cell phone or a favorite blanket):

_____

_____

_____

_____

_____

_____

_____

_____

_____

_____

_____

_____

_____

_____

_____

Rituals (like walking your dog or texting your friend every day):

_____

_____

_____

_____

_____

_____

_____

_____

_____

_____

_____

_____

_____

_____

_____

_____

_____

_____

_____

_____

_____

_____

_____

_____

_____

_____

_____

_____

_____

Food (like chocolate or mac 'n' cheese):

_____

_____

_____

_____

_____

_____

_____

_____

_____

_____

_____

_____

_____

_____

_____

_____

_____

_____

_____

_____

_____

_____

_____

_____

_____

_____

_____

_____

_____

_____

Places (like your room or church):

_____

_____

_____

_____

_____

_____

_____

_____

_____

_____

_____

_____

_____

_____

_____

_____

_____

_____

_____

_____

_____

_____

_____

_____

_____

_____

_____

People (like your best friend or your grandparent):

_____

_____

_____

_____

_____

_____

_____

_____

_____

_____

_____

_____

_____

_____

_____

_____

_____

_____

_____

_____

_____

_____

_____

_____

_____

_____

_____

Activities (like biking, reading, or listening to your iPod):

My thoughts...

About the
Author

Susan Carrell, RN, MS, LPC, is a therapist in private practice in Allenspark, Colorado. Previously, she was the Episcopal Chaplain for Missouri State University and Drury University. She was a substance abuse counselor for adolescents in an inpatient treatment facility and a psychiatric nurse clinician for hospitalized adolescents. She has been the owner and director of a state-certified alcohol and drug education program for youth. She also facilitated groups for high-risk adolescents in public high schools. She is author of *Group Exercises for Adolescents: A Manual for Therapists* (Sage, 1st ed., 1993; 2nd ed., 2000), *The Therapist's Toolbox: 26 Tools and an Assortment of Implements for the Busy Therapist* (Sage, 2001), and *Escaping Toxic Guilt: Five Proven Steps to Free Yourself From Guilt for Good* (McGraw-Hill, 2008). Visit her websites at www.carrellcounseling.com, www.escapingtoxicguilt.com, and www.almostfreetherapy.com.

About the Illustrator

Jack Wiens, MA, LPC, is a freelance artist who works in a variety of media. Jack is also a licensed professional counselor and presents workshops and classes on personal growth and self-care. Visit his website at www.jackwiens.com.

Supporting researchers for more than 40 years

Research methods have always been at the core of SAGE's publishing program. Founder Sara Miller McCune published SAGE's first methods book, *Public Policy Evaluation*, in 1970. Soon after, she launched the *Quantitative Applications in the Social Sciences* series—affectionately known as the "little green books."

Always at the forefront of developing and supporting new approaches in methods, SAGE published early groundbreaking texts and journals in the fields of qualitative methods and evaluation.

Today, more than 40 years and two million little green books later, SAGE continues to push the boundaries with a growing list of more than 1,200 research methods books, journals, and reference works across the social, behavioral, and health sciences. Its imprints—Pine Forge Press, home of innovative textbooks in sociology, and Corwin, publisher of PreK–12 resources for teachers and administrators—broaden SAGE's range of offerings in methods. SAGE further extended its impact in 2008 when it acquired CQ Press and its best-selling and highly respected political science research methods list.

From qualitative, quantitative, and mixed methods to evaluation, SAGE is the essential resource for academics and practitioners looking for the latest methods by leading scholars.

For more information, visit **www.sagepub.com.**